Organizing Guide for Local Unions

George Meany Center for Labor Studies

by
Virginia R. Diamond

LABOR'S HERITAGE
·PRESS·

ISBN number: 0–9633128–0–4
Organizing Guide for Local Unions

DESIGN BY MARTY ANDERSON DESIGN
PRINTED BY DeLANCEY PRINTING

TABLE OF CONTENTS

Organizing the unorganized has always been the driving spirit behind the labor movement.

In earlier years, workers who tried to form unions were beaten by company thugs or shot at by government troops. Union organizers risked—and sometimes gave—their lives to win the fight for dignity and justice on the job.

It is because of the sacrifices of these heroic men and women that American workers enjoy the standard of living we have today.

As we near the end of the century, organizing continues to be the labor movement's vital mission. The anti–union attacks take different forms, but they are just as intense and brutal as in the early days of the labor movement.

Union–busters now carry brief cases instead of brass knuckles, but their aim is the same: to divide and demoralize workers, to prevent them from having a voice on the job and in society.

Despite the setbacks, trade unionists today are no more willing to give up the struggle than were our predecessors.

Workers know that hazards on the job maim and destroy thousands every year. Workers know that discrimination and favoritism rob people of opportunities for advancement. Workers know about inadequate health benefits that threaten the well–being of their families. Workers know about the lack of dignity that exists when people are denied a voice in their working lives.

And trade unionists understand that everything we have achieved can be taken away if we don't continue to organize. Employers pit one group against another, demanding concessions in order to be "competitive." To be strong, we must be united.

Organizing is the job of every single union member. It is the responsibility of all of us to educate our friends and neighbors about what a union really is.

That a union is more than just a collective bargaining agreement. It is more than the improved wages and benefits that come with a union contract. A union is more than the leadership and staff—the lawyers, negotiators, educators, economists—who assist us.

The union is the people themselves, joining together in a triumph of hope over fear, standing up together for justice.

SETTING UP AN ORGANIZING PROGRAM

Although the national or international union provides support, the local union is at the center stage of the organizing effort. How does a local union begin to establish an organizing program?

- **Leadership commitment.** It first takes a commitment on the part of the leadership, a vision of what the union can and should be. Making organizing a priority requires hard choices; it means giving up other things to devote the necessary time and resources to organizing.

- **Membership support.** Next, the leadership must gain the support of the membership for pursuing an aggressive organizing agenda. Illustrate how contractual gains and industry standards can only be maintained and improved if there is a high degree of organization in the industry. Explain the historical importance of organizing the unorganized as the means of building the labor movement. Describe the importance of organizing in increasing the political influence of workers on national and state legislation.

- **Planning.** Third, construct a plan. Analyze the resources of the local union— both financial and membership—and make some decisions on the following issues:
  - ▲ *Resource allocation.* Make available funds to pay for lost time for volunteer organizers or to hire full time staff.

6

▲ *Strategic targeting.* Think about how to expand within your industry. Use collective bargaining and political leverage to achieve fair organizing conditions.

▲ *Involve all facets of the union.* Enlist the support and participation of all staff and activists on behalf of the organizing effort.

■ **Form a Volunteer Organizing Committee (VOC).** Recruit and train a cadre of volunteers—called "VOC's" or "member organizers." Appoint a chair of the VOC. Have regular meetings and give regular reports to the local union. Volunteer or member organizers play a critical role in organizing. They can contribute to the success of your local union's organizing program in many ways, including:

▲ Making home visits to non–union workers

▲ Getting organizing leads from friends and relatives

▲ Attending rallies

▲ Doing library research on non–union employers

▲ Hosting meetings of non–union workers

▲ Making phone calls

▲ Handing out leaflets

▲ Making contact with community groups

Union members make the best organizers, the most credible teachers of non–union workers. Union members know from experience and in their hearts what a union is all about.

■ ***Actively seek leads.*** The local union should have an ongoing active program of meeting and talking with non–union workers. Use the media and public events to raise awareness of the need for organizing in the community. When a collective bargaining agreement is reached, use this as an opportunity to inform people about the union. At community events, state fairs, etc., raise the issue of organizing. Invite the public to attend union educational programs or social events.

■ ***Link up with community groups.*** Form alliances with community, civil rights, women's, senior, church, and other groups. Use these contacts to find organizing leads, as well as to gain support for organizing efforts.

■ ***Give recognition*** for organizing efforts. Use union meetings, newsletters, bulletin boards, to recognize the efforts of VOC's. Have special dinners or banquets to demonstrate appreciation for those who have devoted time to organizing.

A successful local union organizing program requires a serious commitment of time and resources. It requires training and an understanding of successful organizing strategies and tactics. And most of all it requires a local union to create a "culture of organizing," a spirit of dedication to the mission of carrying on the torch passed to this generation by previous generations of trade unionists.

This booklet describes in a general way the phases of a typical organizing drive, suggesting certain guidelines and principles in conducting an effective campaign. Of course, there is in a sense no "typical" campaign; each one is different, and calls upon the organizers to make judgments and resolve dilemmas about how to proceed.

The following chapters raise some of the issues which arise in the different stages of an organizing drive. Below are the phases of a typical organizing campaign:

- **Getting Leads.** This is the ongoing process of identifying and meeting individuals who might be interested in trying to form a union.

- **Research.** Organizers learn as much as possible about the non–union employer in order to determine whether a successful campaign is feasible.

- **List–building.** This is the necessary process of assembling names and addresses of the non–union workforce so that the union can communicate with the workers.

- **Forming an Organizing Committee/One–on–One Outreach.** By meeting with individuals in the workforce on a one–on–one basis—often through home visits—the organizer answers questions about the union, gets information about the workforce, and identifies individuals who might be willing to join an organizing committee.

■ **_Meetings._** The campaign surfaces with organizing committee meetings, where organizers and committee members develop strategies for the campaign, and where committee members are educated about the union.

■ **_Sign–up._** This is the attempt to sign up a large majority of workers on authorization cards or petitions.

■ **_Campaign for recognition_** of the union. Alternative strategies are available for winning recognition from the employer. One approach is to petition for an election before a public agency or the NLRB, and to begin an election campaign. Other approaches to gaining recognition include campaigns that result in the employer submitting to a "card check," in which a neutral third party counts the signatures to determine that majority support exists. Workers can also conduct a strike for recognition. Support from community groups or public officials can be critical in marshalling pressure on the employer to acknowledge that a majority of workers want the union.

■ **_Organizing for a first contract._** After the union wins recognition, the organizing process continues during the period leading up to the first collective bargaining agreement.

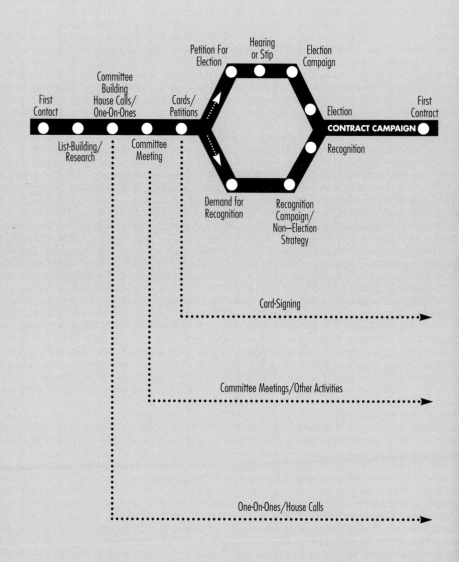

CHAPTER 1

Getting Started

Every organizing campaign begins because one person decides to step forward and try to make changes at his or her job.

It is the task of the local union to identify and contact as many such individuals as possible. Many local unions look strategically for leads at the other facilities in their industry, which, if organized, would enhance the bargaining strength of all workers in the industry.

Getting leads requires ongoing effort. Don't sit back and wait for the phone to ring. Instead, reach out to workers who want to change conditions at work, but who don't know where to go for help.

■ ***Ask your members.*** The most effective way of developing organizing leads is through the membership. Ask members for the names and addresses of friends, neighbors, and relatives who are unrepresented. Shop stewards can canvass their members for leads. Asking people one–on–one is always better than simply sending out a questionnaire to members asking for leads.

It often makes sense to begin a campaign among workers who come into contact or have some relationship with your members. Seek leads from non–union parts of the same workplace or employer. Talk to the workers your members deliver to, receive from, phone or get called by. Make contact with people who work for subcontractors of your employers.

■ *Union visibility.* Make it easier for non–union workers to find you. Local unions can place ads in phone books or newspapers, or on radio. Wherever your union has a visible presence, at state fairs or in parades, take the opportunity to give out a brochure or leaflet and to talk to people about organizing.

■ *Link organizing to union successes.* When you announce a contract settlement in the news media, or run an issue campaign in the community, use the occasion to draw a link to the need to organize new work sites.

■ *Call on community allies for help.* Churches, civil rights organizations, senior groups, are all sources of organizing leads.

In the past, unions often looked for organizing leads by leafleting non–union facilities. Although this might work once in a while, this sort of handbilling can cause lots of problems for any future campaign. Why? Handbilling alerts management to the presence of the union, and can cause the employer to launch an immediate anti–union campaign. Management speeches and letters can intimidate and confuse people, making it more difficult for the organizers to reach the people later. For this reason, it is usually wise to get leads without making it obvious to the employer.

How do you decide whether or not to initiate a campaign? Basic research will allow organizers to make an informed decision. Here are some of the questions to ask:

■ ***Does the facility have a strategic importance for the union?*** Many unions adopt a targeting strategy which strengthens the bargaining power of their organized units, by organizing non–union facilities which are undercutting the ability of unionized companies to pay fair wages and benefits. Not only are you helping non–union workers, you are helping organized workers maintain good pay and benefits. Non–union operations within the organized company offer strategic advantages. The local can use its bargaining strength to gain employer neutrality and a card check during the campaign.

■ ***What is the labor relations history?*** What were the results of previous organizing efforts? Did the employer make promises during the campaign that have since been broken? What type of anti–union campaign did the employer wage? Why did the union lose? This information can be invaluable to the union in designing a strategy to win. It is also important to know whether other facilities within the company are organized.

■ **_Are there strong issues to organize around?_** There must be a certain level of discontent for a campaign to be viable. Be sure that the issues affect a majority of workers, not just a single department or shift.

■ **_Can the local union get a contract and effectively service the unit?_** The facility should be geographically close, and the union should have some knowledge of the industry. Does the local have the necessary leverage to get a contract? Is support available from other organized units within the facility, from other unions, from allies in the community?

An employer should be healthy enough to be able to afford the improvements that people want. There are a number of sources for this type of information. Your international research department may be able to help obtain a range of documents such as annual reports or filings with the Securities and Exchange Commission or the IRS. Check with the state corporation commission, private directories such as Standard and Poor's or Moody's. Look in newspaper files or trade publications.

■ **_Is the unit an appropriate size for your local to organize?_** Large units require the availability of several staff or volunteer organizers. It is better to take on a small unit and win than to try to organize a large unit without the necessary resources. On the other hand, some locals try to avoid getting mired in campaigns at tiny units with just a few workers.

■ **_Do you have strategic advantages, such as a complete list of names and addresses?_** The availability of a list can enable the union to readily contact the workers within a short period of time by mobilizing a large group of house callers. This makes it more difficult for the employer to give misinformation to the people before the union has a chance to talk to them.

WHAT IN BLAZES WAS THAT?!

IT WAS THE WORKERS, SIR. THEY'RE PUTTING THE MOVEMENT BACK IN THE LABOR MOVEMENT!

'85 HUCK/KONOPACKI LABOR CARTOONS

Getting information about a company or agency is important before starting a campaign. But the most important information is the most basic: the names and addresses of the workers.

Without a list of names and addresses, the union has virtually no means of telling the union message. If we had equal access with the employer to the workers, such a list would not be so critical. Assembling a list of names and addresses should take place during the early stage before the campaign goes public. The primary way of building this list is by working with a small number of union supporters in the facility. This list can be supplemented by using phone books and city directories (reference books which list individuals' places of employment).

Since list–building can be laborious and time–consuming, it should not be left until later in the campaign. Having an accurate list of names and addresses—preferably of a large majority of the workforce—enables the organizers to contact people quickly, and to keep the campaign moving ahead.

SAMPLE LIST

Name	Address
Jose Armenta	105 Washington St
Pamela Armstrong	910 5th St. #2
Barbara Dickenson	1233 Mitchell Dr.
Mary Ann Dieux	55 Newman Ave.
Pete Edwards	3301 8th St. #35 (has moved)
Lisa Fabian	8712 River Rd.
Jerome Fisher	8253 Hurley Ave. #??
Brian Graham	3211 Chiswell Dr.
Abdul Hamidiz	54 17th St. #6
Jeffery Holborn	??
Benjamin Houston	234 Wisconsin Ave.
Betty Jones	43 Linden St. #44
David Leinhardt	5630 E. Warner Ave.
Eduardo Lopez	1332 Parklawn Dr.
Gordon Massey	12907 Bushey Dr. (no longer at address)
Penny Matthews	1429 Briars St.
Brendan McMillan	4807 Foxgate Dr.
Maria Mitri	257 Sunnyview Dr.
Jonathon Miyashiro	4112 Coldstrom Pl.
Lynn Novak	??
Patricia November	10973 Bonafint Dr. #19
Neville Platter	7080 Market St.
Artie Robinson	864 Eldsworth Ave. #??
Elliott Segel	7434 Euclid Blvd. moved?
James Stein	8769 Poplar Way
David Senadad	980 Lincoln Pl.#27
Kelley Thorpe	10639 Hammer Rd.
Dawn Tsagaris	12 Tre...
William Whitby	
Aaron Williams	
Anthony Zankel	

CHAPTER 2

House Calls/
One–On–One
Communications

An essential feature of a successful organizing drive is one–on–one communication between the organizers and the workers. Studies of campaigns have revealed that face–to–face, individual conversations are critical. Workers do not commit themselves to the challenge of forming a union based upon literature or phone calls; this commitment comes from a sense of trust and confidence in the organizers and in themselves.

In most organizing situations the organizer cannot carry on this one–on–one communication at the worksite. Therefore, house calls are an indispensable part of most campaigns.

House calls serve many different purposes. Early in the campaign, home visits are used to recruit an organizing committee and learn about the facility. The organizer can find out who the potential leaders are among the workforce, educate them about the union, and invite them to become part of the organizing committee.

Later in the campaign, organizers make house visits to people who have signed cards, to people who are undecided, or to people who are waivering in their support for the union.

Before each house visit the organizer should have an agenda in mind. Here is a typical agenda for house visits early in the campaign:

■ ***Introduction.*** The organizer should introduce him or herself and explain the reason for the visit. For example, "I am _____ from the _____union. Some of your co–workers contacted us because they were interested in making some changes at work. We agreed to visit some people to try to learn a little more about conditions at your workplace. May I come in for a minute?"

■ ***Ask about the worker's issues and concerns.*** Each worker will have a different perspective on conditions at work. Let the worker discuss a range of issues before talking about the union itself. Get to know the person you are talking to before making your points.

■ ***Educate the worker*** about the union. Relate the union to the worker's concerns. Explain how a union would help. Describe the process of organizing a union. Prepare the worker for what management is likely to say or do during a campaign. It is helpful to ask people what they know about unions—remember, many people know very little or have misinformation about how unions work.

- ***Get information.*** If the person is supportive of the union, and wants to help, ask for information about who the leaders are among the workers. Get additional names and addresses of people who should be visited.

- ***Get a commitment.*** Each house call should build the organization in some way. If a person is sympathetic, try to get him or her involved, either by attending a meeting, joining the committee, or doing some other important job. When you leave, raise the issue of a return visit.

USE VOLUNTEER (MEMBER) ORGANIZERS

Union members are the best organizers, and are especially valuable house callers. They are visiting people in their own community, and they can speak from experience about how a union works. By training members to make house calls, you will create a cadre of credible and dedicated individuals. Role–play home visits with the volunteers, so people feel confident about what to say and do. Negotiate a release for volunteers on lost time during periods of intensive house calling.

■ *Limit visits to 30–40 minutes,* so that more people can be seen. You can always continue conversations on later visits.

■ *Don't call ahead.* Setting up appointments can be cumbersome and difficult to adhere to. You are a thousand times more likely to have a face to face conversation if you just drop by. If the time isn't convenient, you can stop by later.

■ *Make full use of your time.* House call from the end of the shift to as late as possible. Have meals before or after house calling hours, so as not to waste valuable time. Saturdays and Sundays after church are good days for visits. Remember, the time spent on home visits may be the organizer's most valuable contribution to the campaign.

■ *Map out directions ahead of time,* so you don't waste time getting lost.

■ *If possible, bring along an inside committee person.* But don't put off visits because a worker isn't available to come along.

■ *Fill out the contact card immediately.*

■ **_Listen._** Don't give speeches. Draw the person out. Let the person talk. Be responsive to the worker's concerns. The best house callers are the best listeners. As long as you are doing most of the talking, you are not getting the responses you need to work with someone effectively. You can give the best speech in the world, but it won't help unless it is heard. The best way to get someone talking is to ask questions. For example, "How do you like the new looms they put in?" "Have they done anything about the dust in the finishing room lately?" "Do you like working on the second shift better than on the third?" People talk about things they know about. If you can get people talking about their jobs, you can have a conversation instead of a sales pitch.

■ **_Don't assume._** You may think you know what the issues are, but frequently you will be surprised. Different issues matter to different people. Again, ask and listen.

■ **_Don't argue._** You are not trying to win a debate or score points. All you do by arguing is make the person defensive. Always try to find points of agreement. Find common ground, then politely suggest other points of view.

■ **_Don't make a sales pitch._** An organizer is not a sales person. A union is not a product. A union is the people themselves.

In order to truly gain a voice on the job, they must join together with their co-workers and stand up for their rights.

■ **Always be honest.** Don't promise what the union can't deliver. Never invent information. People respect honesty, not arrogance. If someone asks you a question to which you don't know the answer, tell them you don't know, but will find out and get back to them. Then, do it.

■ **Involve family members.** The support of parents or spouses will be critical as the campaign progresses. Be friendly and relational; show people you are interested in them.

CONTACT CARD

NAME _____   SHIFT _____ JOB _____

ADDRESS _____   TELEPHONE _____

_____   DATE OF HIRE _____

CONTACTED ON_____**BY**_____

ISSUES IDENTIFIED_____

CONCERNS EXPRESSED_____

ASSISTANCE OFFERED_____

UNION SUPPORT   −   ?   +   (circle one)

COMMITTEE   YES   NO   (circle one)

COMMENTS_____

_____

The "blitz" is a strategy which calls for an extensive use of volunteer organizers to visit workers at their homes during a very short period of time at the start of a campaign. For example, 30 volunteer organizers could visit nearly 200 workers during a two day "blitz." This can give organizers a chance to talk to people before the employer has had a chance to intimidate them through "captive audience" meetings or letters.

To employ a "blitz" strategy, the union needs an accurate list of names and addresses, as well as a large group of trained volunteers. Typically, the purpose of the visits is to recruit an organizing committee, invite people to a union meeting, and sometimes to sign cards.

HOUSE CALLS RESULT IN MORE WINS

When organizers make home visits, the union win rate goes up. A survey shows that when the organizer house calls between 60 and 75% of the unit, the win rate is 78%. If the organizer makes no house visits, the win rate is 41%. Attempts to communicate with employees indirectly can impact unfavorably on the win rate. In campaigns where the union relies on letters to communicate with workers, the win rate is only 39%. When organizers use the telephone as a key means of campaigning, the win rate is only 40%.

SOURCE: AFL–CIO ORGANIZING SURVEY

Here are some typical questions asked during home visits and some issues raised by employers during anti–union campaigns, and some suggested responses. The answers will vary among different unions, but here are some samples.

Q *What will be in our contract?*

A It is for the employees to decide what to negotiate for. After you win union recognition, you will elect a negotiating committee from among your co–workers. This committee will survey the workers to see what you want in your contract. Then, with the assistance of union negotiators, the committee will sit down with management to negotiate a contract.

The law says that both sides must bargain "in good faith" to reach an agreement on wages, benefits, and working conditions. The contract will only take effect after it is approved (ratified) by a majority of the workers.

It is not possible to know exactly what will be in the first contract. Our goal will be to win improvements with each contract.

Q *Who runs the union?*

A The union is a democratic organization run by the members. You will elect your own officers. You vote on all issues of importance to you. You vote on your contract. Union members elect delegates to national conventions, where delegates elect officers and vote on major issues affecting the union such as constitutional amendments. The union is the people themselves.

Q *Won't it cost the employer a lot money if the union comes in?*

A In the short run it's true that unions cost employers more in terms of wages and benefits. But in the long run, that doesn't necessarily hurt the employer. Many unions are good for the employers as well as for the workers.

The reason is simple. With a union there is higher morale, and there is a mechanism for workers to have a voice in how the workplace operates.

Satisfied employees are more productive, and less likely to quit, so there is less turnover. Also, management benefits when it gets input from the workers on how the operation could be run better.

Q *Can I be fired for participating in the campaign?*

A First of all, the law prohibits the employer from discriminating against people in any way because of their union activity. If an employer does harass or discriminate against a union supporter, the union files a charge with the Labor Board, and prosecutes the employer to the fullest extent.

The best safeguard against the employer harassing anyone is for everybody to stick together and win their union. Without a union, management has a free hand to treat people as they please. But with a union, everyone has the protection of a union contract.

Q *What can the union do about favoritism?*

A Fairness is the most important part of the union contract—the same rules apply to everyone. If any worker feels that he or she is not being treated fairly, then he or she of course still has the opportunity to complain to the supervisor, just like before. But under a union contract, the supervisor or manager no longer have the final say. They are no longer judge and jury. If the worker is not satisfied with the response of the supervisor, the worker can file a grievance.

The first step of a grievance procedure is for the steward to accompany the worker to try to work it out with the supervisor. If the worker is not satisfied, the steward and the employee can bring the grievance to higher management. If the complaint is not resolved, then the issue can be placed before an outside neutral judge, called an arbitrator.

Q *The employer is spreading the rumor that we could lose the benefits we now have. Is that true?*

A The purpose of forming a union is to win improvements in wages and benefits, not to lose them. We start with what we have and go up. On average, unionized workers earn a third more than non–union workers in wages and benefits. Occasionally in organized facilities workers agree to grant concessions to aid an ailing company, but this comes after years of winning improvements.

The employees vote on whether or not to accept a contract. Would you vote to accept a contract that took away your benefits? Think about it. If having a union meant that the employer could reduce your benefits, why would the employer be fighting the union so hard?

Besides, it is against the law for the employer to retaliate against the union by taking away wages or benefits.

Q *What about all these articles and speeches the employer has been giving about the union being corrupt?*

A The employer would like you to think that unions are corrupt. The truth is that unions are decent, honest organizations dedicated to improving the lives of working people.

Nothing is perfect, and there have been examples of union officials who have not been honest. But the same is true of government officials and business leaders.

Telling you not to vote for a union because there have been some corrupt officials is like telling you never to work for a company because some company officials are corrupt.

Q *The employer says the union can't guarantee us anything. Can you?*

A The union can guarantee this: that when workers stick together as a union they have more bargaining power and more of a voice than they do as individuals.

When the union wins, you will negotiate a contract with the employer. We can make no promises on what the contract will contain—that is for you to decide when you vote on your contract. We can guarantee that the contract will be legally binding, and the union will make sure the contract is enforced.

Q *The employer is implying the company could close if the union came in.*

A Companies do not go out of business because they have a union, or because the workers are treated fairly. Companies close because of market conditions or poor management. This is a scare tactic that employers use to keep people from gaining a voice on the job. We researched this company, and last year the profit was _____.

More non–union companies close each year than unionized companies. Government studies have shown that a unionized firm is no more likely to close than any other company.

With a union contract, fair wages and working conditions, and a voice on the job, workers here will be more productive, and the company will probably do better, not worse.

Q *Management says the union is just after our dues money. Why should we pay money to the union?*

A In this union the dues are ____ per month. No worker will pay any dues until after a contract has been negotiated by your elected committee and voted on (ratified) by a majority of workers. It doesn't cost, it pays, to be a union member.

The dues are divided between the local union and the national union. The money is used to provide expert services to the local union, including negotiators, lawyers, economists, educators; to pay the salaries of officers and staff, including organizers; to provide newsletters and conferences. The local union's money is used for reimbursing stewards for lost time, for the union hall, and for other expenses of the union.

Did you know that the employer also pays dues to organizations? Employers have their own "unions" such as the Chamber of Commerce or the National Association of Manufacturers. They pay for representation—why shouldn't you?

Besides, since when is the employer so concerned about where you spend your own money?

Q *Management says there will be a strike if we organize.*

A Management talks a lot about strikes during an organizing drive. But did you know that over 98% of union contracts are settled without a strike? There could only be a strike if the employees vote for the strike. And it's only smart to vote for a strike if you know you can win. The employer doesn't want a strike any more than the workers do, so everyone has an incentive to reach a compromise during bargaining.

Unions have developed a lot of other tactics that can put pressure on management to reach a fair agreement. For example, unions use boycotts or corporate campaigns or community support, rather than necessarily having to resort to striking.

Q *How do we go about getting a union here?*

A The first step is to form a committee among the workers with representatives from each department. The committee's job is to attend meetings and educate themselves about the union. Then they can educate their co–workers, and help to dispel false information spread by management.

Next, the majority of employees must sign cards (or a petition) stating that they want to have a union here. After a majority of workers have signed up, we can ask the employer to recognize the union, or file a petition for an election.

If we file for an election, then we will have a chance to vote in a secret ballot election for the union. If the union wins a majority of votes, and the employer does not challenge the vote on legal grounds, then we can begin the process of negotiating a collective bargaining agreement.

 What does signing this card mean?

A It means you want the union. Please do not sign just to get an election. The card is a commitment of support.

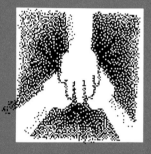

CHAPTER 3

The Organizing Committee

An active, representative organizing committee is the most important element in a successful campaign. It is the foundation upon which a strong union is built.

The inside organizing committee provides the leadership and inspiration to win and sustain majority support among the workforce. These are the people who are in the workplace every day, combating management lies and rumors, teaching people what a union really is, showing people that they don't have to be afraid to stand up to management.

Except in very small units, the organizer cannot talk to every worker on a daily basis. But the organizer can be in daily contact with the committee. And the committee can be in daily contact with the rest of the workforce. So with a committee, the face–to–face communication so necessary to win is possible.

The organizing committee has a number of critical functions during the campaign:

- **Provides leadership.** By openly supporting the union, the committee provides leadership and inspiration to the rest of the workers. Committee members take part in planning the campaign, and in carrying out union activities.

- **Conveys a sense of ownership.** Since the committee consists of the workers themselves, workers get a greater sense of ownership of the union. The union is not some outsiders; it is the people themselves.

- **Educates co–workers.** At committee meetings, committee members learn more and more about the union. They bring this information to their co–workers. They can respond to management misinformation as soon as it appears.

- **Serves as a communication network.** Committee members are the eyes and ears of the organizer in the workplace. They can tell the organizers what is happening in the campaign, what the issues are, and what people's concerns are.

- **Acts as a watchdog.** The committee keeps records of threats or other legal violations committed by the employer. Committee members know their legal rights, and can share this information with others.

■ ***Distributes literature and signs up co–workers***. The committee is responsible for giving out leaflets to the workers, and are usually the ones who sign up the workers on union cards or petitions. The fact that the committee members give out the leaflets shows workers that they don't have to be afraid to engage in union activities.

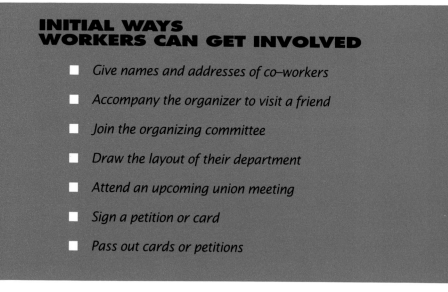

INITIAL WAYS
WORKERS CAN GET INVOLVED

- *Give names and addresses of co–workers*

- *Accompany the organizer to visit a friend*

- *Join the organizing committee*

- *Draw the layout of their department*

- *Attend an upcoming union meeting*

- *Sign a petition or card*

- *Pass out cards or petitions*

In putting together an effective committee, the organizer should keep these guidelines in mind:

■ **Size.** The committee should consist of at least 15% of the workforce. If the committee is much smaller, they cannot be a visible presence on the job, communicating with everyone in the workforce on a daily basis.

■ **Representative.** Every department, work area, shift, and job category should be represented on the committee. Every ethnic and racial group, age group, and both genders should also be reflected on the committee, so no worker feels left out. Everyone should have someone on the committee he or she knows and can identify with.

■ **Leaders.** People who serve on the committee should be well–respected, solid workers. They should be the natural leaders whom others admire.

It is the job of the organizers to create this committee through one–on–one recruitment. Seek out leaders who represent every segment of the workforce. Even if a person is not initially pro–union, make the effort to show the person how a union can address their concerns.

Don't just recruit people who are the most pro–union at the outset. This may not be the most representative group. Organizers sometimes make the mistake of spending most of their time with the strongest union supporters. Instead, immediately seek out those areas of the workforce where union support may be weak. These areas may mean the difference between winning or losing the campaign.

Don't surface too early with a partial committee. If the committee is too small, or not fully representative, it will present the wrong face to the rest of the workers. People may get the impression that the union is a clique and not strong enough to inspire their co–workers. Don't call your first meeting too soon.

One critical decision organizers have to make is when or whether to inform management who is on the organizing committee. The argument for sending the employer a letter with the names of the committee members, or for putting their names on a leaflet, is twofold. It solidifies the committee, and it offers some legal protection— the employer cannot deny knowledge of who is on the committee.

A committee cannot be effective if it stays hidden. Once the committee is ready to surface, take them into action with a leaflet distribution.

Remember to keep adding members to the committee throughout the campaign. The committee should grow in strength and diversity.

The more workers involved in the campaign, the more likely you will succeed in winning recognition, securing a first contract, and building a healthy local union that will remain strong for years to come. The main way you recruit people as active participants in a campaign is by explaining that there will only be a union if they work to create one, and take ownership of the process. Also:

■ **Ask.** The best way to get someone to do something is to ask him or her personally. This is infinitely more effective than trying to recruit through a mailing or phone call.

■ **Make clear** what job you are asking people to do. People are more willing to begin with things they know they can do. When they accomplish something, they are more confident, and will participate more next time.

■ **Encourage** people to ask questions. Remember that most people have never been through an organizing campaign before and that they don't know what tasks are involved or what is meant by "leafletting," or "house calling."

■ **Tell each person** how his/her job fits in with the rest. People want to understand what they are a part of, and they work best when they know that others are depending on them.

■ ***Start small and build.*** The first time, ask someone for three addresses and phone numbers. Don't ask them to find 150 addresses in two days—they will probably fail and you will lose a potential activist. People will be more willing to do more as their confidence builds.

■ ***Keep people accountable.*** At each meeting, check and see if and how the person did the assignment. This sends the message that the work is important, and helps to identify problems early.

■ ***Explain*** how their work will help make people's lives better. Be enthusiastic about the importance of the work. People will work hard and take enormous risks if they truly believe they can make a difference.

THE COMMITTEE IS THE KEY

The most significant factor leading to union success is active campaigning by an effective, representative committee. In the absence of an effective committee, the win rate is only 10%. When the organizing committee does engage in active campaigning the win rate is 62%.

A committee of less than 5% of the unit correlates to a win rate of only 27%. But of the committee consists of 15% of the unit or more, the win rate is 61%.

SOURCE: AFL–CIO ORGANIZING SURVEY

Once all or most of the committee has been recruited, committee meetings can begin. These meetings typically take place every week. Some tips for effective meetings include:

■ *Have an agenda.* The purpose of the meeting should be clear. It should not turn into a gripe session or pep rally. The purpose is to answer questions, train, and conduct the work of the campaign, which includes inoculating workers against the employer campaign, assessing union support, determining strategy, etc.

■ *Keep the meeting short.* Start and end on time. Meetings should not last longer than one hour. Otherwise, people with family and other responsibilities will

SAMPLE COMMITTEE MEETING AGENDA

5:00   *Report on anything new in the workplace*

5:05   *Report results of previous assignments*
           Give recognition to people who did their
           assignments

5:10   *Discussion of next phase of the campaign*
           (for example, education on authorization cards—purpose,
           who sees them, signing a card as a commitment of support)

5:20   *Role play by committee of next assignment*
           (for example, members practice soliciting cards from
           co-workers)

5:50   *Assignments–Distribution of cards.*
           (for example, each worker may agree to talk to five specific
           co-workers about signing cards)

6:00   *Adjourn*

stop coming. If people want to talk longer, let them stay after the meeting and talk.

■ ***Meet at a convenient time*** and a neutral place. Avoid lounges and restaurants that might make some workers uncomfortable or be too noisy. Offer child care if possible.

■ ***Encourage participation.*** Nothing will kill committee interest faster than prolonged speeches. Instead, suggestions, discussion and participation by committee members will keep them interested and eager to make their contributions to the success of the campaign.

Two principle components of your committee meeting are training and assignments. Often they overlap. For example, if the committee is about to begin soliciting union authorization cards, part of the meeting is spent explaining what the card means, and preparing for conversations with co–workers about the cards. The best way to prepare for this or other activities is to role–play with the committee. Let people on the committee role–play the co–worker or the committee person, and let the "worker" raise the questions likely to come up. That way, committee members can help each other produce the best answers and approaches.

The assignment phase of the meeting would involve dividing up the cards, and deciding who is going to recruit which co–workers, as well as deciding when and where the cards should be turned in.

It can be a challenge to create a unified majority in a culturally diverse workforce, especially since standard employer practice is to divide and conquer. To build an effective organization, the committee must represent all groups within a diverse workforce and the union must address issues that unfairly impact one group or another.

Here are some ideas for trying to create a unified workforce:

■ **_Identify the leaders_** of different groups and make it a priority to make early contact with them. Make sure the committee is fully representative.

■ **_Don't delay in reaching out to every cultural group._** If the organizer waits until the campaign is under way to visit and reach out, some groups may get the impression that the union is the property of others.

■ **_Take advantage of community resources_** for contacts and translations. Whenever possible, house calls should be conducted in someone's primary language.

■ **_Be sure to translate all literature._** Show that the union cares about everyone.

■ **_Be sensitive to cultural traditions,_** and avoid offending people with certain values or beliefs.

It should not have to be said, but we will anyway: organizers should always conduct themselves in a non–sexist, non–racist manner. The union should not become a social club for any exclusive group, majority or minority.

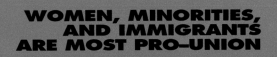

WOMEN, MINORITIES, AND IMMIGRANTS ARE MOST PRO–UNION

A large proportion of female workers in a unit significantly increases the union's chance of organizing success. In units where women make up less than half of the workforce, the win rate is only 33%. Where women equal more than 75% of the unit, the union's win rate is 57%. More than half of union election victories feature a workforce with a majority of women.

Unions have the greatest chance of success if the workforce is more than 75% minority. If there are large numbers of immigrants in the workforce, there is a strong likelihood of success. Such units have a win rate of 63%.

SOURCE: AFL–CIO ORGANIZING SURVEY

CHAPTER 4

Labor Law

Workers have the legal right to organize, and it is against the law for employers to discriminate against employees for exercising this right.

This right is contained in several laws which cover different groups of workers. The National Labor Relations Act establishes the legal framework for organizing and collective bargaining in the private sector. The federal sector is governed by the Federal Labor Relations Act. Railway and airline workers are covered by the Railway Labor Act. And state, county and municipal workers are granted rights under various state and local laws, as well as under the Constitution.

The rights granted to workers under these various laws are similar. This chapter will discuss the National Labor Relations Act in particular.

As anyone involved in organizing campaigns knows, there are many problems with the National Labor Relations Act. Penalties against employers who violate the law are very weak. And employers can abuse the process by seeking lengthy delays. Nevertheless, it is important for organizers and committee members to understand the basic protections offered by the law, and to know how to prosecute employers under the law.

The National Labor Relations Act ("NLRA") declares that the policy of the United States is to encourage "the practice and procedure of collective bargaining and (to protect) the exercise by workers of full freedom of association, self–organization, and designation of representatives of their own choosing, for purposes of negotiating the terms and conditions of their employment or other mutual aid or protection."

The following are some of the specific rights workers have under the NLRA. (Note: These are general legal principles, and exceptions can occur.)

■ ***"Talking Union" and Soliciting Union Cards.*** Workers have the right, as a general rule, to campaign for the union and solicit union cards during non–work time. In most situations workers can "talk union" even in work areas, although there are exceptions in some industries such as retail and health care. If workers are allowed to have casual conversations about non–work topics during work, then they are also allowed to talk about the union during work. The right to solicit for the union also applies to wearing union buttons and insignia.

■ ***Distributing Union Literature.*** Workers have the right to distribute union literature during non–work time in non–work areas, such as break rooms and cafeterias.

- **Surveillance.** Employers may not spy on union activities, or create the impression of surveillance.

- **Interrogation.** Employers may not interrogate workers about their union sympathies if the worker wants to keep his or her opinions private.

- **Threats.** Employers may not threaten workers with retaliation for union activity. It is unlawful to threaten to take away benefits or close a facility to punish workers for organizing.

- **Discrimination.** Employers are prohibited from discriminating against workers in any way because of their union sympathies or activities. This includes suspensions, discharge, transfers, or demotions.

Undocumented workers are covered by the protections of the National Labor Relations Act.

If an employer violates the National Labor Relations Act, this is called an "unfair labor practice" (ULP). The union or an individual can file a charge with the National Labor Relations Board (the "Labor Board") when such a violation occurs. (See sample charge form.)

Within a few weeks of receiving the charge, the Labor Board will send in an agent to investigate the charge. The union must assemble all of its evidence at this time to present to the Board agent. This includes bringing together any witnesses who can support the charge by giving a statement to the Board agent.

Members of the inside organizing committee should keep notes of all incidents or conversations that might be unfair labor practices. Such records of exact dates, times, and places of threatening statements are important to present a complete case to the Board. (See sample committee ULP notes.)

After interviewing union witnesses, the Board agent will talk to the management to get its side of the story.

After the investigation is complete, if the Labor Board finds merit in the charge, it will issue a complaint, and prosecute the employer. If the Labor Board does not find enough evidence to support the charge, the charge may be dismissed.

CHARGE AGAINST EMPLOYER

GPO : 1984 O - 435-440

FORM NLRB-501
(8-83)

FORM EXEMPT UNDER 44 U.S.C. 3512

UNITED STATES OF AMERICA
NATIONAL LABOR RELATIONS BOARD
CHARGE AGAINST EMPLOYER

DO NOT WRITE IN THIS SPACE	
Case	Date Filed
14RX-10632	4/7/92

INSTRUCTIONS: File an original and 4 copies of this charge with NLRB Regional Director for the region in which the alleged unfair labor practice occurred or is occurring.

1. EMPLOYER AGAINST WHOM CHARGE IS BROUGHT

a. Name of Employer	b. Number of workers employed
SOMEWHERE INDUSTRIES	110

c. Address (street, city, state, ZIP code)	d. Employer Representative	e. Telephone No.
1529 12th St, Scott City, KS. 63021	William Jones	601-773-1212

f. Type of Establishment (factory, mine, wholesaler, etc.)	g. Identify principal product or service
MANUFACTURING	WIDGETS

h. The above-named employer has engaged in and is engaging in unfair labor practices within the meaning of section 8(a), subsections (1) and (list subsections) 8 (a) 3 _____ of the National Labor Relations Act. and these unfair labor practices are unfair practices affecting commerce within the meaning of the Act.

2. Basis of the Charge (be specific as to facts, names, addresses, plants involved, dates, places, etc.)

The employer, in order to discourage membership in a labor organization, discriminated in regard to the hire and tenure of employment and to the terms and conditions of employment of the following named employees on and after dates set opposite their names

Susan Smith   March 29, 1992
John Watkins   March 30, 1992

By the above and other acts, the above-named employer has interfered with, restrained, and coerced employees in the exercise of the rights guaranteed in Section 7 of the Act

3. Full name of party filing charge (if labor organization, give full name, including local name and number)

ABC Union, AFL-CIO

4a. Address (street and number, city, state, and ZIP code)	4b. Telephone No.
809 A Street, Scott City, KS. 63021	601-766-9876

5. Full name of national or international labor organization of which it is an affiliate or constituent unit (to be filled in when charge is filed by a labor organization)

6. DECLARATION

I declare that I have read the above charge and that the statements are true to the best of my knowledge and belief.

By _Michael Phillips_ (signature of representative or person making charge)   Representative (title if any)

Address _PO Box 416, St. Louis, MO 54321_   601-789-5486 (Telephone No.)   6/6/91 (date)

WILLFUL FALSE STATEMENTS ON THIS CHARGE CAN BE PUNISHED BY FINE AND IMPRISONMENT (U. S. CODE, TITLE 18, SECTION 1001)

COMMITTEE INCIDENT REPORT

1. Date of Incident _January 2, 1992_

   Time of Incident _11:30 am_

   Location of Incident _Department C_

   Description of Incident _Supervisor John Lester said to Maria Hernandez "You'll be sorry you signed a card when you apply for a promotion."_

   Witnesses _Alfredo Smith_

2. Date of Incident _____

   Time of Incident _____

   Location of Incident _____

   Description of Incident _____

   _____

   _____

   _____

   Witnesses _____

   Name of Committee Person _Mary Jones_

In order to gain union recognition and certification under the National Labor Relations Act, the union must prove it has the support of a majority of the workers. One way of gaining union certification is through the Labor Board election process. This is how the process works.

A union which believes it has majority support files a petition for an election with the Labor Board. In support of its petition the union must present to the Board authorization cards or petitions from at least 30% of the workers. (Note: These cards are sent to the Labor Board, not to the employer. The Labor Board does not show these cards to management.)

Before holding the election, the Labor Board decides which job classifications are eligible to vote. The classifications which will be included in the "bargaining unit" are determined either through an agreement between the union and management (a "stipulation") or through a formal hearing. There are certain rules about what constitutes "an appropriate unit" under the National Labor Relations Act. (see page 60) The election takes place on average about 50 days after the petition is filed, although it can be a shorter or longer period.

The vote itself is a secret ballot election conducted by the Labor Board, usually at the worksite. The employer is not allowed to present a "captive audience speech" within 24 hours before the election. No electioneering is allowed at or near the polls, and union supporters may not keep lists of who has voted. The union must get 50%+1 of the votes in order to win.

Within seven days following the election, either side may file objections based on the other party's conduct during the period up to and including the election.

Organizers must consider questions concerning the make–up of the bargaining unit. The Labor Board has evolved a number of general rules, as well as some special rules that apply to certain industries, such as hospitals.

The following are a few issues about which organizers should be aware:

- **Multiple locations.** Generally, if the establishment has separate, autonomous facilities, each run by a single manager, each facility can have its own bargaining unit. However, if the facilities are geographically close, run from a central location, with a lot of interchangeable employees, the Board may find a company–wide or multi–site unit to be appropriate. Some industries have special rules regarding multiple sites.

- **"Community of interest."** In determining the eligibility of each job category to vote in an election, the NLRB will examine various aspects of the job. A general principle the Labor Board uses is the concept of "community of interest." If workers share common supervision, common working conditions, common benefits, and come in contact with each other or are interchangeable, they are likely to be included in the same unit.

- **Professional employees** may not be included in a unit of

WHAT WILL THE BETTER PAID, BETTER PROTECTED PROFESSIONALS BE WEARING NEXT YEAR?...

non–professionals unless the professionals vote to join the unit.

■ ***Temporary employees*** are included in the unit if they have a "sufficient likelihood of continued and permanent employment."

■ ***Regular part–time employees*** are normally included in the unit. Laid–off workers are in the unit if, looking at all the relevant facts, the Board determines that there is a reasonable expectation of recall in the foreseeable future.

■ ***Office clerical workers*** are not included in a unit of production or service workers, whereas "plant clericals"—clericals whose work does not relate to administrative matters and who work closer to the rest of the workforce—are included.

■ ***Supervisors are not eligible*** to become part of a bargaining unit. Supervisors also do not enjoy the protection of the National Labor Relations Act, and they can be disciplined or discharged if they are supportive of the union effort.

It can be difficult to determine exactly who qualifies as a supervisor under the National Labor Relations Act. Often there are disputes as to whether lead workers are in or out of the unit.

The law defines a supervisor as someone who has the authority to "hire, transfer, suspend, lay off, recall, promote, discharge, assign, reward, or discipline other employees, or to effectively recommend these acts." These supervisors must act with "independent judgment," not merely carry out the decisions of others in a routine or clerical manner.

In many cases, people think they are supervisors because they have a supervisory title. But a person's title does not determine whether or not he or she is a supervisor under the law.

People who may be supervisors should not serve on the union committee or solicit union cards. Solicitation of union cards by a supervisor is grounds for overturning an election.

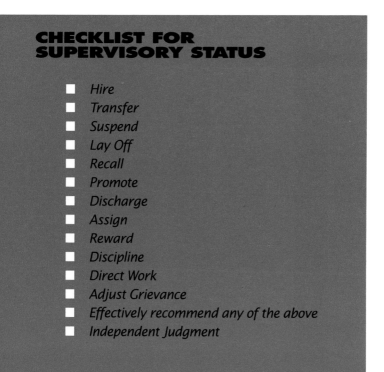

CHECKLIST FOR SUPERVISORY STATUS

- ■ *Hire*
- ■ *Transfer*
- ■ *Suspend*
- ■ *Lay Off*
- ■ *Recall*
- ■ *Promote*
- ■ *Discharge*
- ■ *Assign*
- ■ *Reward*
- ■ *Discipline*
- ■ *Direct Work*
- ■ *Adjust Grievance*
- ■ *Effectively recommend any of the above*
- ■ *Independent Judgment*

■ ***Card Check.*** The employer may agree to voluntarily recognize the union without the necessity of an election. Under a "card check" agreement, the signed cards or petitions are given to a neutral outside party, such as a member of the clergy or public official. If the outside third party concludes that a majority of workers have signed for the union, then the employer agrees to recognize the union and begin bargaining.

■ ***Bargaining Order.*** In rare cases the Labor Board will order the employer to recognize and bargain with the union without an election, if management has committed such pervasive and egregious unfair labor practices that a fair election is impossible. Called a "Gissel order," such a bargaining order will only occur if a majority of workers have signed for the union.

■ ***Recognitional Strike.*** Workers may go on strike to demand union recognition. Within 30 days of going out on strike, the workers are required to file a petition for an election.

After a union wins certification, the employer has a duty to bargain in "good faith" for a collective bargaining agreement. Management is required to meet at reasonable times and places, and provide the union with information needed for bargaining.

Management is not allowed to make any unilateral changes in wages or working conditions without first bargaining over these changes. However, previously scheduled raises and benefit improvements cannot be withheld while negotiations take place. The employer is not required to freeze pay and benefits during bargaining.

CHAPTER 5

Sign–Up

An essential goal of the organizing effort is to gain signatures from a large majority of workers on either authorization cards or petitions. Studies show that the union needs to sign up between 65% and 75% of the unit to be likely to win. These signatures can be used either to get an election, or for "voluntary recognition" through a card check.

Although the National Labor Relations Board only requires that 30% of the unit sign cards to get an election, organizers insist on having a large majority, because support can erode as the employer wages a fierce "Vote No" campaign.

PETITION FOR THE UNION

We the undersigned hereby declare that in order to achieve fairness on the job we authorize the _____ union to represent us for the purposes of collective bargaining.

There are two types of authorization cards: single purpose cards, and dual purpose or membership cards. The single purpose card serves as a "showing of interest," but is not a membership card. The dual purpose card is also a union membership card. Some unions include a dues check–off provision in the card as well.

While the majority of campaigns feature the signing of cards, some organizers use petitions instead. Proponents of this method argue that it creates additional momentum as workers see their co–workers sign the petitions, and signing a petition requires a more open commitment than signing a card.

_____UNION AUTHORIZATION CARD

We believe that only through collective bargaining can we have a voice in our work place, achieve fair treatment for all, establish job security and fair benefits, wages and working conditions. Therefore, this will authorize the _____ Union, AFL-CIO, to represent me in collective bargaining with my employer.

PLEASE PRINT:

_____
NAME

_____
EMPLOYER NAME   DATE

_____
ADDRESS

_____
CITY   STATE   ZIP   PHONE

_____
SHIFT   DEPARTMENT

_____
SIGNATURE

NOTE: This authorization to be signed and dated in employee's own handwriting. Your right to sign this card is protected by Federal Law.

Organizers must make the judgment whether to start signing people up from the start of the campaign or to wait until after the organizing committee has been formed. The main argument for signing people up early is that it is a test of commitment from early union supporters. The main reason to wait and start the sign up later is that there can be a tendency to focus on getting cards signed, rather than on building the committee.

It can be a strategic advantage to have the card or petition sign–ups take place over a short time, rather than spreading this stage out over many weeks. If the sign–up phase takes too long, early signers can get discouraged and wonder why the campaign isn't going faster. If the organizer holds off on signing people up until there is a strong committee, there can be a sense of excitement and momentum as everyone signs up.

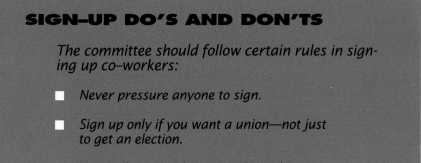

SIGN–UP DO'S AND DON'TS

The committee should follow certain rules in signing up co–workers:

■ *Never pressure anyone to sign.*

■ *Sign up only if you want a union—not just to get an election.*

■ *Keep asking people to sign throughout the campaign.*

CHAPTER 6

Record Keeping

Methodical record–keeping is one of the most important jobs of the union organizer. Without good records, it is impossible to make correct decisions about strategy and tactics.

Every organizer should assemble and continually update the following information:

■ ***Name and Address List.*** The names and addresses of unit employees are the most vital tools an organizer can have in order to effectively communicate with the workers. Working with committee members and other sources, organizers should have a list early in the campaign. The list should include anyone who may or may not end up being included in the unit. An organizer should never be in the position of waiting for an "Excelsior List" (which the employer must provide 10 days before the election) to know who is in the unit. It is useful for organizers to divide the name and address list by department, in order to assess union support and to ensure that the committee is representative.

■ ***Worksite Chart.*** The organizer should, again with the assistance of the committee early in the campaign, develop a chart of the worksite, drawing in each worker. This chart is useful for several reasons: to visualize the union's strengths and weaknesses, to be sure that work areas and departments are not overlooked, to identify who the supervisors are, and to become aware of the proximity and interactions of various work groups.

■ **_Contact Cards._** The organizer should maintain a card file with a contact card for each worker. Every time a worker is visited, notes can be made on the visit. Locations of the homes can be written on the back.

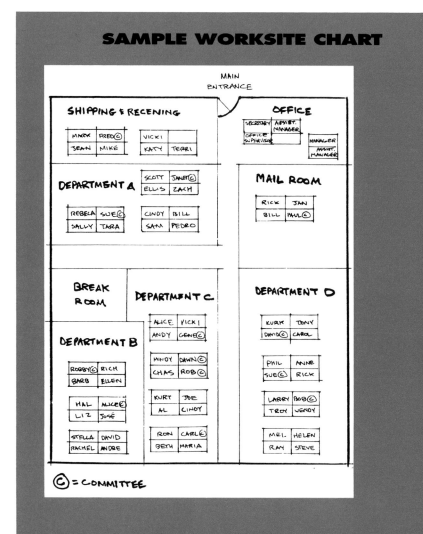

SAMPLE WORKSITE CHART

MAIN ENTRANCE

SHIPPING & RECEIVING

MARK	FRED Ⓒ		VICKI	
JEAN	MIKE		KATY	TERRI

OFFICE

SECRETARY	ASSIT. MANAGER
OFFICE SUPERVISOR	

MANAGER

ASSIT. MANAGER

DEPARTMENT A

SCOTT	JANET Ⓒ
ELLIS	ZACH

REBECA	SUE Ⓒ		CINDY	BILL
SALLY	TARA		SAM	PEDRO

MAIL ROOM

RICK	JAN
BILL	PAUL Ⓒ

BREAK ROOM

DEPARTMENT C

ALICE	VICKI
ANDY	GENE Ⓒ

DEPARTMENT B

ROBBY Ⓒ	RICH
BARB	ELLEN

HAL	ALICE Ⓒ
LIZ	JOSÉ

STELLA	DAVID
RACHEL	ANDRE

MINDY	DAWN Ⓒ
CHAS	ROB Ⓒ

KURT	JOE
AL	CINDY

RON	CARL Ⓒ
BETH	MARIA

DEPARTMENT D

KURK	TONY
DAVID Ⓒ	CAROL

PHIL	ANNE
SUE Ⓒ	RICK

LARRY	BOB Ⓒ
TROY	WENDY

MEL	HELEN
RAY	STEVE

Ⓒ = COMMITTEE

Computerization of records can be useful during some organizing drives, particularly in large units. Computers help generate information, for example, on who lives in which zip code, which can help in giving out house call assignments. They can tell you if there are certain groups within the workplace that you are not reaching. Organizers should keep in mind that computerizing records can mean much time–consuming data entry.

Organizers have their own systems for indicating worker sentiment towards the union. An effective assessment system takes a "snapshot" of union support at a given time. Keeping track of people's likely votes is important in order to focus time and attention on people who are wavering or undecided. It can also tell the organizer how to progress to the next stage of the campaign by using existing support effectively. Assessments are taken continually through every organizing campaign because people's opinions, issues and support change as the campaign progresses.

For example, in the early phase, you need to know if there is potential for a campaign in a workplace. The goal of your assessing system during this phase is to find out how many people support the idea of a union at the workplace. An effective system will tell you whether or not you have sufficient support to begin signing up workers without ever having given out one card.

Assessments of people's attitudes towards the union should be based on objective criteria where possible, not only what people tell the committee or the organizer. Did the person sign a card? Has the person been to meetings? Have they provided any assistance to the union? Is he or she publicly for the union? Which people have influenced this person and who does he or she influence?

Union organizers often make the mistake of spending their time talking to die–hard union supporters, instead of focusing on people leaning either for or against the union. It is this middle group of people who will decide whether there will be a union. That's why accurate assessments are so critical in determining who needs to be visited and what issues need to be emphasized.

SAMPLE DEPARTMENT LIST

DEPARTMENT LIST
Northville Nursing Center
Work Area List
Week 2

KEY:

LPN = Practical Nurse	**X** = Card Signer	**1** = Strong Yes
NA = Nurse's Aide	**C** = Committee	**2** = Leaning Yes
WC = Ward Clerk		**3** = Leaning No
DA = Dietary Aide		**4** = Strong No

NURSING A WING - 1st Shift

Name	Title	Card	Assessment	Committee
Susan Wilson	LPN	X	1	C
Lucy King	LPN		4	
Dennis Woods	NA		3	
Pat Oakes	NA	X	2	
JoAnn Monroe	NA		3	
Linda Ross	NA	X	1	
Debbie Turner	NA	X	1	C
Terry Otis	NA	X	1	
Nancy Hiller	NA	X	2	
Adele Cohen	NA	X	2	
Jennifer Norton	WC		4	

NURSING B WING - 1st Shift

Name	Title	Card	Assessment	Committee
Ben Zucker	LPN	X	2	
Marion Steward	LPN		3	
Sharon McGregor	NA	x	1	
Linda Griffin	NA	X	2	
David Dahn	NA		3	
Dawn Landers	NA	X	2	
Janelle Overton	NA	X	2	
Nancy Frost	NA	X	1	C
Mara Corley	NA	X	1	C
Sylvia Jeffreys	NA	X	2	

CHAPTER 7

The Employer Campaign

Workers who seek to improve their lives by forming a union on the job are almost always in for a fight.

Typically, management likes things as they are, where they call all the shots. So they spend a lot of money to hire anti–union consultants—experts who earn their living trying to keep working people from earning a decent living.

When the anti–union consultants come on the scene, they pretty much take over. They write speeches for management to deliver at "captive audience" meetings (ie., meetings workers have to attend while they are on the clock.) They draft letters which management signs and sends to workers' homes. They draw up leaflets which are handed out on the job. They train supervisors on how to talk against the union. They use "dirty tricks" and gimmicks, spread rumors, and show films.

Even though the union–busting consultants are writing the script, the workers will probably never see them, except perhaps as they sneak in and out of the office. They stay backstage, watching as the mayhem unfolds.

Many anti–union consultants are lawyers, who can use legal maneuvering to cause delays in the process. They figure if they delay long enough, workers will get too discouraged to stick together. Besides, the meter is running.

The typical employer campaign is a two–headed monster. There is the "nice guy" approach. Supervisors smile and ask how you are. Promises are made. Raises are given. Unpopular supervisors disappear. Complaints are resolved.

Don't underestimate how effective this approach can be, especially when the manager tearfully promises to be better and begs for one more chance. He can promise anything he wants—after all, this "niceness" only has to last until the end of the campaign.

Then there is the campaign of fear. Supervisors warn workers they will lose their benefits if they form a union. Management threatens to close the facility, to force people out on strike. News clippings shriek of union–inspired violence. Union officials are portrayed as greedy bosses only interested in dues money.

Some consultants like to use gimmicks. Like a split paycheck, with the dues money taken out. Or a grocery cart filled with items that could be purchased with a year's dues money. Some employers give prizes to the worker who can guess the number of days lost to strikes. Tombstones line the path outside the facility with names and dates of plant closings. Supervisors give workers "guarantee booklets" with coupons for organizers to sign.

Real work almost grinds to a halt, as supervisors spend the day bending workers' ears, trying to talk them out of supporting the union. Management even entices some workers to form their own "anti–union committee," to spread rumors against the union and wear "VOTE NO" buttons.

Just when workers think they've heard everything, management usually saves up a last–minute "bombshell"—often a tale of some strike or plant closing somewhere.

All of these distortions and lies about unions are designed for one purpose: to make workers forget why they wanted a union in the first place. The employer hopes people will get so sick of the pressure that they will just want the union to go away.

Some of these tactics are legal, some aren't. Often management is so eager to beat the union that they don't mind bending the law when necessary.

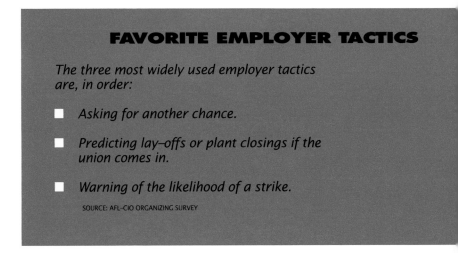

FAVORITE EMPLOYER TACTICS

The three most widely used employer tactics are, in order:

- ☐ *Asking for another chance.*

- ☐ *Predicting lay–offs or plant closings if the union comes in.*

- ☐ *Warning of the likelihood of a strike.*

SOURCE: AFL-CIO ORGANIZING SURVEY

Union–busting consultants are vicious. But they can be beaten, and they are beaten by workers every day.

One thing to remember is that they are extremely predictable. When the organizers and inside committee members are prepared, and tell the workers what to expect, management tactics lose their sting.

■ ***Predict.*** If you suspect the employer will use a particular tactic, be sure to educate your committee. This gives you credibility. Predict both the fear tactics and the "nice guy" approach. "Inoculate" the workers, by telling them what management will say before they say it.

■ ***Pre–empt.*** Knowing what to expect from the employer campaign, the union can go on the offensive and take some of their issues away from them. For example, a health care employer often falsely accuses the union of being indifferent to patients; go on the offensive by campaigning from the start for better patient care.

■ ***Involve workers.*** The most effective response workers can give to almost any management claim is, "It is our union. We make the decisions." Don't just tell the workers that they are the union; show them, by involving them in decision–making during the campaign.

■ ***Take credit for improvements.*** By spelling out early in the campaign what improvements the union will fight for, you are in a better position to take credit for improvements management makes during the campaign. "If we got 50¢ an hour more just by talking about the union, imagine what we can make with a contract."

■ ***Stay on the offensive.*** Stick to your issues. If you get stuck continually responding to management's campaign, you will lose. Management talks continually about the futility of organizing. You need to provide the hope that conditions can change.

Nurses. . .
Who Loses in a Strike?

Families LOSE income
for running the household. . .

Hospitals LOSE respect,
and sometimes patients. . .

Employees LOSE income,
and sometimes their jobs

Only the union organizers
have nothing to lose be___ their
income contin___

Let's help each___

January 1___
Vote NO

✓

Strikes!   Strikes!   Strik___

IS THIS THE UNION ID___
OF JOB SECURITY
171 Strikes in Only One Ye___

Millions of dollars in lost wages due to Union strikes!
DON'T RISK ANY LOSS OF INCOME
Vote No!

GET THOSE UNION PROMISES

To protect against rash promises by
certain union promises GUARANT___
official sign and date each of the ___

I Guarantee: you will get a pay
raise of _____ cents an hour in the
very first contract we get with you___
company.

Signed_____ (Official Organizer)_____ Date_____

I Guarantee: that the Consti___
and By-Laws of the Union d___
include trials and penalties ___
members.

Signed_____ (Official Organizer)

I Guarantee: the unic___
the support of your f___
their expenses if yo___
of work because of ___
the union.

Signed_____ (Official Orga___

I Guarantee:___
hourly rate c___
the first day___
event you___
because ___

Signed_____ (___

I Gua___
a re___
unic___

Sig___

82

Membership in the union will cost YOU money...

Dues
Fees
Fines
Assessments

Janua...
Vote N...

THIS IS WHAT THE UNION WANTS FROM YOU

WE NEED YOUR—

✗ INITIATION FEES
✗ MONTHLY DUES
✗ FINES
✗ ASSESSMENTS
✗ STRIKE CONTRIBUTIONS

"UNION BOSS"
HE WANTS YOUR MONEY!

VOTE NO ✗ SAVE YOUR DOUGH!

...

...: your ri...
...f with your co...
...will not be rep...
...rolled process.

...d   (Official Organizer)

I Guarantee: that th...
who become union...
other local union offi...
receive super-senior...
...tection over you in th...
...lay-off.

Signed   (Official Organizer)

5

...our
...with
...e
...work
...rikes.

I Guarantee: if you a...
strike you will get yo...
the end of the strike,...
whether you have be...
nently replaced by y...

Signed   (Official Organizer)   Date

8

...e
...7

...not have
...ts in the

I Guarantee: there will be no lay-
offs regardless of whether or not
your company has work to do.

Signed   (Official Organizer)   Date

10

Date

9

...ION ORGANIZER HAS SIGNED EACH COUPON, YOU SHOULD VOTE NO!

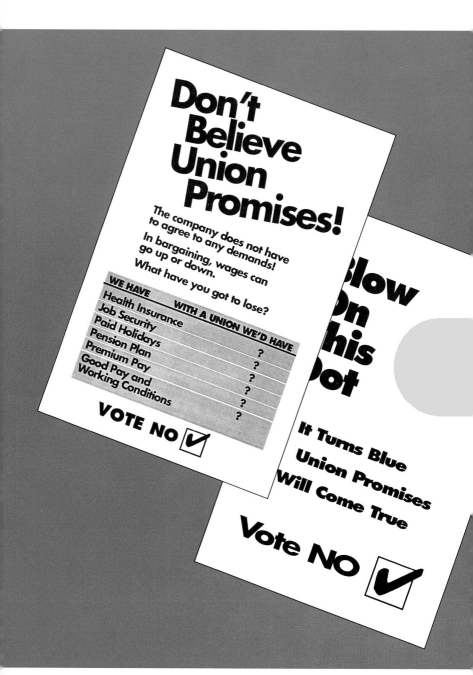

Don't Believe Union Promises!

The company does not have to agree to any demands! In bargaining, wages can go up or down.

What have you got to lose?

WE HAVE	WITH A UNION WE'D HAVE
Health Insurance	
Job Security	
Paid Holidays	?
Pension Plan	?
Premium Pay	?
Good Pay and Working Conditions	?
	?

VOTE NO ☑

...low on this Dot

It Turns Blue
Union Promises
Will Come True

Vote NO ☑

EVEN IF YOU SIGNED A CARD YOU CAN STILL VOTE NO!

JANUARY 18TH VOTE NO

Lightning isn't the only thing that strikes!

Let's help each other.

Jan. 18th Vote NO

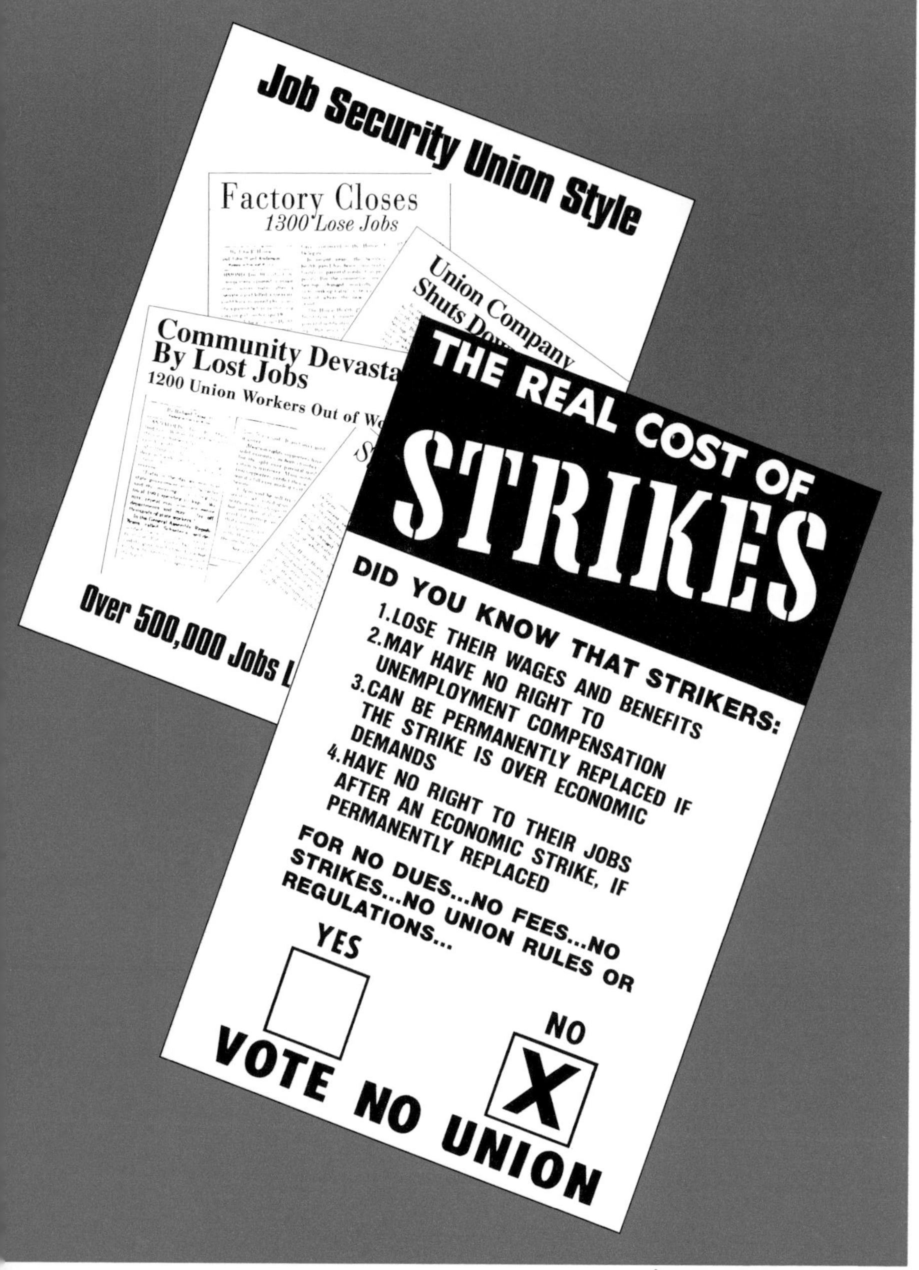

Job Security Union Style

Factory Closes
1300 Lose Jobs

Union Company
Shuts Down

Community Devasta
By Lost Jobs
1200 Union Workers Out of Wo

Over 500,000 Jobs L

THE REAL COST OF
STRIKES

DID YOU KNOW THAT STRIKERS:
1. LOSE THEIR WAGES AND BENEFITS
2. MAY HAVE NO RIGHT TO
UNEMPLOYMENT COMPENSATION
3. CAN BE PERMANENTLY REPLACED IF
THE STRIKE IS OVER ECONOMIC
DEMANDS
4. HAVE NO RIGHT TO THEIR JOBS
AFTER AN ECONOMIC STRIKE, IF
PERMANENTLY REPLACED

FOR NO DUES...NO FEES...NO
STRIKES...NO UNION RULES OR
REGULATIONS...

YES ☐

NO ☒

VOTE NO UNION

CHAPTER 8

Communications

Union literature offers the organizing committee and others a chance to come forward publicly in support for the union. Signed by the committee and distributed openly, this material can help keep union issues out front. Here are some tips for effective leaflets.

- **Keep them simple.** Don't try to cover too many issues. Make your main points in bold type.

- **Image is important.** Avoid misspellings, sloppiness, and inaccuracies. This literature reflects the image of the union.

- **Involve the committee.** Often the most important thing for workers is not what the leaflet says, but who hands it out. Committee members should hand out flyers.

- **Timing.** Be ready to give out flyers on a moment's notice if an issue is hot. For example, if there is a captive audience meeting, or if the employer corrects a problem or does something which angers people, use a leaflet to interpret the event immediately.

- **Don't be defensive.** In general, it is a mistake to respond in writing to the employer's charges. Stick to your positive agenda. Use the verbal network of the committee to respond to employer attacks.

■ **_Appeal to moderates._** Be positive, and direct the literature towards people who are not sure where they stand. Don't simply preach to the converted. Stridency only appeals to people who already agree with the union message, and can alienate others.

■ **_Be creative._** Use humor. Find the artists, poets, cartoonists, humorists, among the workers and involve them.

■ **_Put the workers out front._** Use workers' pictures and statements in the literature. Again, the message is "we are the union."

There are some fun ways to defuse the employer campaign. Popcorn on the day of an anti-union movie. Fortune cookies with a pro-union message. If the facility is not air conditioned, hand out pocket thermometers. Find creative ways of demonstrating the union's position on an issue.

During the campaign you always try to involve "moderates"—those workers who are somewhat pro-union or undecided. Petitions about a popular issue and stickers addressing a widely felt concern are low risk ways of beginning to involve people in the campaign and building solidarity. You must know ahead of time, however, that most workers will participate so that your activity won't backfire. Petitions, stickers, "wearing thermometers around your neck to protest poor heating" can build momentum and demonstrate solidarity only if your support looks strong.

Buttons, t-shirt, stickers, hats. Use your props to build solidarity and add momentum. But watch out for putting buttons or hats on too early—then if management succeeds in taking off even one person's button, you get a reverse momentum.

It's important to be creative, and use humor. An imaginative display is often more powerful than a grim and negative message. Humor and fun also dispel the employer's phony ploy that the union is a hostile, divisive force that wants to hurt the employer.

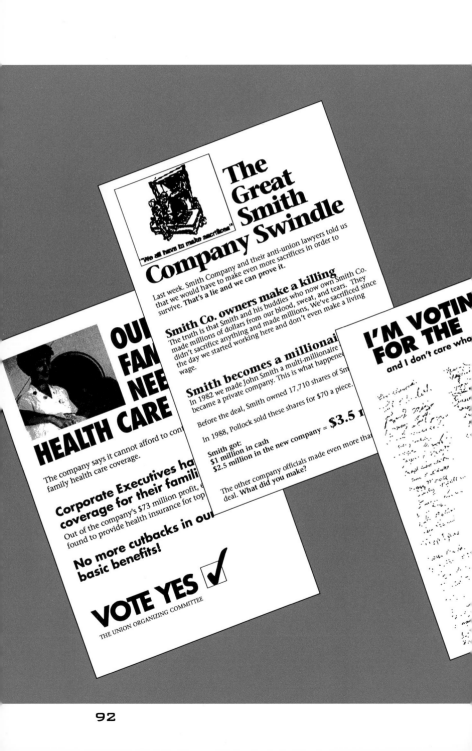

The Great Smith Company Swindle

"We all have to make sacrifices"

Last week, Smith Company and their anti-union lawyers told us that we would have to make even more sacrifices in order to survive. **That's a lie and we can prove it.**

Smith Co. owners make a killing

The truth is that Smith and his buddies who now own Smith Co. made millions of dollars from our blood, sweat, and tears. They didn't sacrifice anything and made millions. We've sacrificed since the day we started working here and don't even make a living wage.

Smith becomes a millionai

In 1982 we made John Smith a multi-millionaire became a private company. This is what happened of Sm

Before the deal, Smith owned 17,710 shares of Sm

In 1988, Pollock sold these shares for $70 a piece.

Smith got:
$1 million in cash
$2.5 million in the new company = **$3.5 r**

The other company officials made even more tha deal. **What did you make?**

OU[R]
FA[M]
NEE[D]
HEALTH CARE

The company says it cannot afford to con family health care coverage.

Corporate Executives ha[ve]
coverage for their famili[es]

Out of the company's $73 million profit, found to provide health insurance for top

No more cutbacks in ou[r]
basic benefits!

VOTE YES ✓

THE UNION ORGANIZING COMMITTEE

I'M VOTIN[G]
FOR THE

and I don't care who

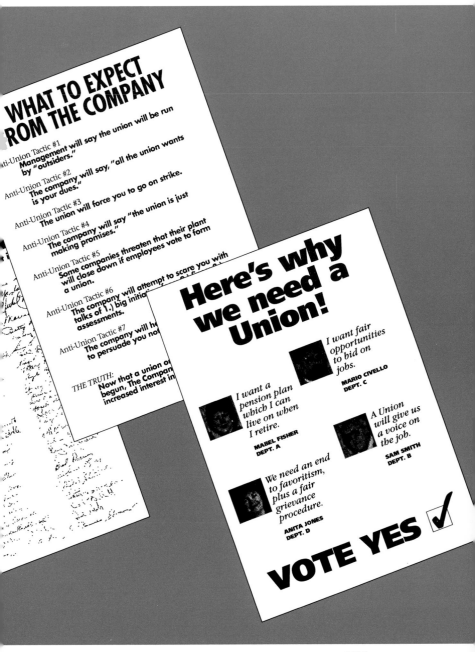

WHAT TO EXPECT FROM THE COMPANY

Anti-Union Tactic #1
Management will say the union will be run by "outsiders."

Anti-Union Tactic #2
The company will say, "all the union wants is your dues."

Anti-Union Tactic #3
The union will force you to go on strike.

Anti-Union Tactic #4
The company will say "the union is just making promises."

Anti-Union Tactic #5
Some companies threaten that their plant will close down if employees vote to form a union.

Anti-Union Tactic #6
The company will attempt to scare you with talks of 1.) big initia... assessments.

Anti-Union Tactic #7
The company will h... to persuade you no...

THE TRUTH:
Now that a union o... begun, The Compan... increased interest in...

Here's why we need a Union!

I want a pension plan which I can live on when I retire.
MABEL FISHER DEPT. A

I want fair opportunities to bid on jobs.
MARIO CIVELLO DEPT. C

A Union will give us a voice on the job.
SAM SMITH DEPT. B

We need an end to favoritism, plus a fair grievance procedure.
ANITA JONES DEPT. D

VOTE YES ✓

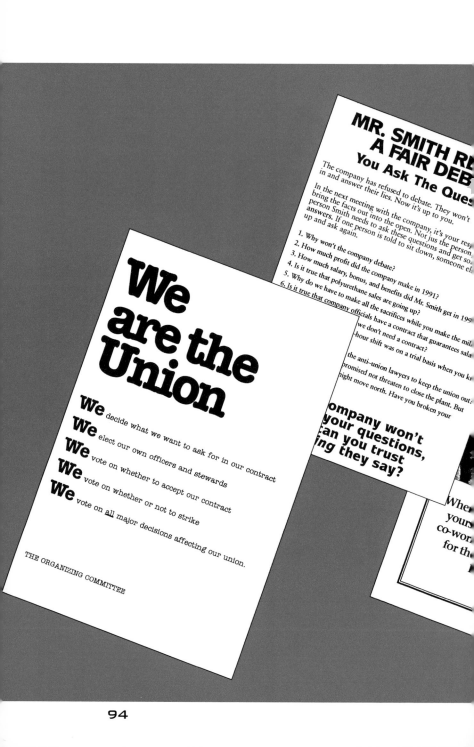

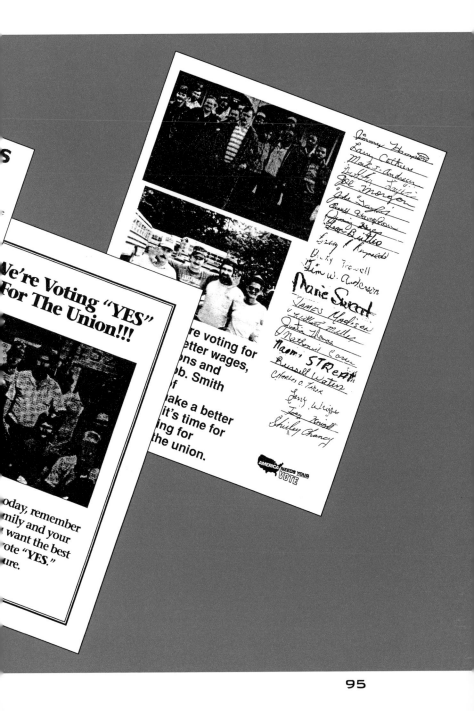

We're Voting "YES" For The Union!!!

...re voting for
...etter wages,
...ons and
...b. Smith

...ake a better
...it's time for
...ing for
...the union.

...oday, remember
...mily and your
...want the best
...ote "YES."
...ure.

CHAPTER 9

Recognition
Through
an Election

There are several different paths to gaining union recognition. Each of them–elections, recognitional strikes, card checks–involves different strategic issues. This chapter addresses some considerations surrounding election day.

The final days of the campaign should create a sense of optimism and excitement. People can talk about what they want in the contract. Prepare a leaflet, meeting, rally or party for election eve.

Organizers must focus on "get out the vote" (GOTV) strategies in the final days. Be sure to build a list of union supporters on leaves of absence, vacation, sick leave or lay–off, and arrange for their transportation to the polls. Phone banks are often effective, especially where workers call their friends and urge them to vote YES.

Management will campaign up until the last moment. Although the "24 Hour Rule" under the National Labor Relations Act prohibits "captive audience" speeches less than 24 hours before the election, supervisors can and do campaign one–on–one. Be ready for last minute tricks including double paychecks (one with the union dues deducted), stories of strikes and plant closings, and pleas for another chance.

The union and the employer can have an equal number of observers (non–supervisory personnel) to monitor the voting. Voters will see observers before they vote. Therefore, choose observers who are popular, respected and representative of the various groups within the unit. You can arrange for rotating observers if there are several shifts, so workers can see someone from their own shift. The most important job of observers is to challenge voters who should not be voting—for example, someone not on the eligibility list or not in the unit, a supervisor, someone no longer employed or someone who started work after the eligibility date.

The Labor Board prohibits electioneering at or near the polls. The Board has a well established rule that election observers are not permitted to keep a list of employees who have or have not voted, aside from the official eligibility list used to check off voters as they are given their ballots.

■ ***Time of Election.*** It is preferable to have the election at the beginning of the shift because supervisors can campaign one–on–one up until the time of the vote.

■ ***Releasing of Voters.*** Supervisors should not be the ones to release the voters because this creates the appearance that the employer, not the Labor Board, is running the election. Options for releasing include: releasing observers; announcements over the public address system (not by a supervisor); or self–releasing through a posted schedule.

■ ***Election Location.*** The Labor Board presumes that the election should be held on the employer's premises. However, under exceptional circumstances an election may be held by mail ballot (eg. where a unit is geographically scattered), or at an off–premises site. The voting booth should not be in a supervisory area.

CHAPTER 10

Campaign Strategy
and Tactics

To win an organizing campaign in the face of intense employer resistance requires a combination of good strategy, adequate staffing, use of volunteers, an effective committee, methodical record–keeping, and hard work.

For each campaign, union organizers develop a strategy uniquely suited for the situation. However, there are certain basic strategic guidelines that are important to keep in mind for every campaign. These include:

- **Use adequate staff and volunteers.** One organizer, or a part–time organizer, cannot handle the demands of a large unit alone. When unions do not assign a sufficient number of staff or volunteers to work on the campaign, they tend to resort to short cuts, such as relying on leaflets or mailings to communicate with the workers. The union has a choice to make: either allocate sufficient resources to organize large units, or stick with small ones.

- **Keep the union campaign quiet** during the information–collecting phase. Don't surface too early with leaflets and meetings. Use this time to quietly build a list of names and addresses, to chart the facility, and to make house calls to the homes of potential committee members. Once the campaign becomes public, the employer is likely to begin creating a climate of fear which will make it harder to reach people.

■ **Build a strong foundation** by forming a large, representative committee. Winning or losing depends often on how well the foundation is built early on, not on what happens during the last week or two. Try to recruit at least 15% of the unit to be on the committee. And give the committee an active role in soliciting cards, handing out leaflets, and educating their co–workers. Keep committee meetings short and to the point. Give out assignments, and hold people accountable.

■ **Move the campaign** as quickly as possible. Caution and procrastination can mean that while the organizer knits at one end, the campaign unravels at the other. Frontload staff and volunteers, rather than bringing in more people later in the campaign. Collect a card majority in as short a time period as possible. The union controls the pace in the pre–petition phase of the campaign; once a petition is filed, we have little control over timing. Again, the extra staff and volunteers early on will help build the committee which will be the foundation that will withstand the inevitable employer assault.

■ **Keep momentum building** by continuing to sign cards or petitions, and keep adding to the committee. Save some activities for late in the campaign, such as wearing buttons and t–shirts. Don't burn out the committee or the workers by having too many meetings early on.

■ **_Make house calls._** Throughout the campaign, go to see card–signers, undecided voters, potential committee members, as many workers as possible. There is no substitute for the one–on–one conversations, away from the workplace, where workers can truly speak openly and have their questions answered. Although there are campaigns where house calls are not necessary, this is the exception rather than the rule. Don't call ahead—just hit the doors.

■ **_Design the campaign_** to appeal to moderate workers. Unless the union has overwhelming support, don't polarize the workforce. In many cases, strident attacks on the employer backfire. Present the union in a positive, not a negative, light. Show a vision of what the union will be. Organizers should not spend all their time talking to supporters or "preaching to the choir." Focus on the middle–of–the–road, undecided workers.

■ **_Plan._** To develop effective strategies and tactics, organizers should discuss the facts with other organizers, and come up with a plan. Good strategies are useless if they are not carried out in a disciplined fashion. Implementation of the strategies requires attention to detail, and plain old drudgery. Hard work and meticulous attention to detail can make all the difference.

Organizers must develop strategies on numerous facets of the campaign, including:

▲ A strategy for getting a list of names and addresses.

▲ A timetable with certain goals in terms of committee size, cards signed; if goals are not met, consider ending the campaign.

▲ A decision on how much staff and how many volunteers will be assigned to the campaign.

▲ A plan for developing issues over the course of the campaign.

▲ Strategies for inoculating workers and preempting employer attacks.

▲ Schedules and topics for meetings.

▲ Decisions on outreach to the community and to the media.

▲ Strategies for using leaflets, both as a way of communicating a message, and as an outlet for committee leadership.

▲ Election versus non–election strategy.

Ultimately, the organizer on the scene has to make judgments about how to run the best campaign possible. Avoid wishful thinking, face facts, and in this way give the workers their best shot at winning the dignity and respect that having a union brings.

In some situations the organizer may make the determination that it would be a mistake to continue the campaign.

Lay the groundwork for this decision by establishing some goals for each phase of the campaign. Involve the committee in setting these goals, and gain the workers' endorsement of a timeline for achieving the goals.

For example, you may have a committee that consists of only 8% of the unit, or there may be certain departments or shifts that are underrepresented. The organizer might determine that unless 10 new committee members are recruited within two weeks, the campaign should be abandoned.

Similarly, a card–signing drive may only yield cards from 48% of the unit. The organizer and committee might decide that unless 40 additional cards could be obtained within three weeks, the campaign should be halted.

If the leadership within the unit understand and accept these goals, it will be easier for the organizer to return at a later date to begin a new campaign when conditions are improved.

General meetings, open to all workers, are a part of many campaigns. In contrast to committee meetings, general meetings should be held sparingly. Many organizers hold one general meeting early in the campaign and one towards the end.

A well–planned, well–attended, and well–run meeting can provide a show of strength, increase the pace of the campaign, and build momentum.

On the other hand, a poorly attended meeting creates a negative momentum. Whatever the reason for the poor attendance, the word goes out that the workers are losing interest in the union.

Don't leave attendance to chance. Know in advance who is coming, and get personal commitments from people to be there. Committee members should know exactly who in their areas will, or will not, attend. Use word of mouth, leaflets, posters, house calls, and all other means to get people there. The location should be convenient and familiar.

Don't use too big a hall. People could feel lonely. A small packed room brings people together.

As with committee meetings, have an agenda and keep the meeting short. People should leave wanting more, not less. Encourage participation; let people ask questions and offer opinions. Don't be defensive about negative questions.

Avoid speech–making. Visiting union officials can offer a brief greeting and no more.

Studies have shown that where attendance at general meetings is 40–50% of the unit, the chance of winning is enhanced. But if the attendance is below 40%, the win rate declines.

Unorganized workers are part of their communities, and organizers should not neglect opportunities to reach out for support and assistance from community groups and leaders during organizing campaigns.

Most local unions already have established alliances and coalitions in their communities, because of work on politics, community services, strike support, and other struggles.

Don't forget to call on these allies for help in organizing. Often the employer calls on its own allies in the community. Local newspaper editorials against the union, business threats of harm to the community if the union wins, even some clergy taking a stand against the union, have harmed worker efforts to win justice on the job.

Environmental, civil rights, senior citizen, women's groups, other labor organizations, central labor councils, churches, can all enhance the public's understanding of the importance of the union organizing effort.

The following are some ways community outreach can help:

- ▲ To develop organizing leads
- ▲ To join on picket lines
- ▲ Mass demonstrations and marches
- ▲ Joint press conferences
- ▲ Petitions to public officials or to the employer
- ▲ Boycotts
- ▲ Leafleting
- ▲ Donations and material support to workers
- ▲ Endorsements by respected community leaders
- ▲ To provide meeting spaces
- ▲ To pressure the employer to bargain in good faith
- ▲ To ask boards of directors to support neutrality during the campaign, or not to hire union–busters

CHAPTER 11

Organizing for a First Contract

If the union loses the campaign, the organizers should lay the groundwork for future attempts. This includes:

- ▲ meeting with the committee
- ▲ showing respect for workers who campaigned against the union
- ▲ holding management to its promises
- ▲ keeping in periodic contact with leaders within the workforce

The campaign is not truly won until a first contract is signed.

The first step after gaining recognition is to reach out to those who did not support the union. Show that you respect their views, and now that the union is here, how important it is to stick together to get the best possible contract. Try to get them to assume leadership positions.

Union supporters should resist the temptation to gloat, or lecture, or demand that the "no" voters get on board. Instead convey the importance of why broad support benefits everyone.

The key to post-recognition or post–election campaigns is to keep organizing. Our goals are: to win a contract, to build a strong enough unit to enforce it, and to win further gains in the future.

Don't make the mistake of dismantling the organizing committee and substituting a tiny negotiating committee, or setting up a hierarchy which keep most people out of the process.

There should be as many or more people involved at this stage as before.

Always aim for maximum participation, particularly from those workers who did not support the union. Get them involved.

If the employer challenges the election or refuses to bargain, don't rely exclusively on legal procedures to force management to the bargaining table. Consider organizing a pressure campaign immediately.

For example, ask workers to sign petitions, attend rallies, wear buttons and hats, confront the boss, etc., to demonstrate the extent of workers support for the union.

- **■** ***Engage in job actions*** to show that the union is getting stronger, not weaker. Use group grievances to pressure management to solve workplace problems.

- **■** ***Aggressively assert*** workers' rights under the law, including health and safety standards, wage and hour regulations, and equal opportunity statutes.

- **■** ***Reach out to the community*** for support. Contact religious leaders and public officials. Use press conferences and demonstrations to mobilize public support.

A general sequence for negotiating a first contract is as follows:

■ *Hold meetings* and conduct one-on-one surveys with all workers to find out what issues they want addressed in their first contract. You may even start these meetings before recognition is won. Everybody likes being asked their opinion, and the committee will gain valuable information to add to what was discussed earlier in the campaign.

■ *Enlist worker participation* in activities supporting those priorities. A visible campaign behind certain bargaining goals increases your power with the employer.

■ *Sign–up as many members* as possible. Be sure to reach out to those who did not support the union.

■ *Conduct an election of a negotiating committee from among all the workers* to represent the union during negotiations.

■ *Begin face-to-face negotiations* with the employer based on the proposals developed.

■ *Reach a tentative agreement* between your committee and the employer.

■ *Bring back that agreement* to all the workers for ratification or rejection by a secret ballot.

Once bargaining has begun, don't neglect the need to continue organizing. Make sure the members are informed of the progress of the negotiations. Plan a series of activities to dramatize the members' support for bargaining issues; for example, if a major issue is health benefits, have everyone wear a button with a slogan about the issue.

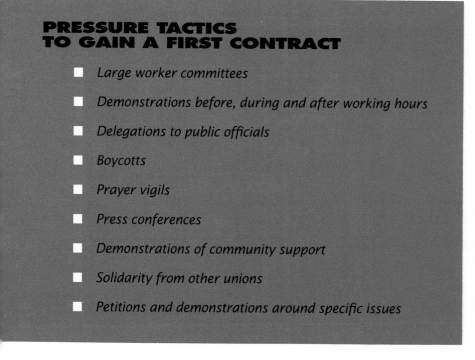

PRESSURE TACTICS TO GAIN A FIRST CONTRACT

- *Large worker committees*

- *Demonstrations before, during and after working hours*

- *Delegations to public officials*

- *Boycotts*

- *Prayer vigils*

- *Press conferences*

- *Demonstrations of community support*

- *Solidarity from other unions*

- *Petitions and demonstrations around specific issues*

■ International/National Union
  Organizing Department

■ George Meany Center for Labor Studies
  (ask about courses on organizing)
  10000 New Hampshire Avenue, NW
  Silver Spring, Maryland 20903
  301 431 6400   FAX 301 434 0371

■ AFL-CIO Organizing Institute
  1444 Eye Street, NW
  Washington, DC 20005

■ AFL-CIO Department
    of Organization and Field Services
  815 Sixteenth Street, NW
  Washington, DC 20006

■ Publications:

  ▲ *ORGANIZING AND THE LAW,* by Stephen
    I. Schlossberg and Judith A. Scott,
    Bureau of National Affairs, Inc.,
    1991.

  ▲ *LABOR LAW HANDBOOK,* by Virginia
    R. Diamond, AFL-CIO Pamphlet
    No. 216.0000.

  ▲ *THE BLITZ,* AFL-CIO Pamphlet
    No. 187-R1089-5.

  ▲ *NUMBERS THAT COUNT,* a manual
    on internal organizing, AFL-CIO
    Pamphlet No. 184.

ACKNOWLEDGEMENTS

The author wishes to acknowledge Richard A. Bensinger, Executive Director of the AFL-CIO Organizing Institute, whose insights based upon his 20 years of organizing experience provide the theoretical underpinnings of this book.

The author also wishes to thank Marilyn Sneiderman of the George Meany Center for Labor Studies for her ideas as well as her tireless efforts in coordinating the production of this book.

Thanks also to the many others who read and commented upon the manuscript, including Paul Booth, Larry Cohen, Mary Ann Collins, Earnie Curtis, Mary Kay Henry, Harold McIver, Allison Porter, Evelina Marquez, Vicki Saporta, Andy Stern, and Louise Walsh.